Mountain Lore

History and Place Names of Mount Diablo

RICH MCDREW AND RACHEL HAISLET

Published by Mount Diablo Interpretive Association

ISBN: 1-978-0-9748925-1-1

Cover photo: site of old Mountain House; see page 92

Book design by Rita Ter Sarkissoff • www.springhillbooks.com
Printed in Korea by www.asianprinting.com

CONTENTS

INDIAN GRINDING HOLES AT ROCK CITY

ROI PEERS

History of Mount Diablo

GEOLOGICAL FORMATION

Upon hiking Mount Diablo, a curious rock formation strikes the eye. Packed into the mountain along Summit Road is a ribbon of brownish-red sediment distinct from the surrounding soil. *What could it be?* Radiolarian chert, a substance formed at sea when the skeletons of tiny radiolarian organisms fell to the ocean floor, decomposed into silica ooze, and solidified. It is part of the Franciscan assemblage, one of three groups of rocks that make up Mount Diablo. Comprising Mesozoic rock, it exhibits the region's unique oceanic history. The other two, Mount Diablo ophiolite and the Great Valley Group and younger sedimentary rocks, also reveal the role of undersea plate tectonics in the formation of the mountain.

How remarkable it is to imagine the towering terrain once submerged. The core of Mount Diablo began taking shape under the Pacific Ocean hundreds of miles away, possibly as far away as the equator, according to geologists. Volcanic rock hardened upon an expanding ocean rift zone, and then a process called *subduction* occurred. As a result of tectonic forces thrusting it northward, the basaltic lava rock was grated and heaped between the Pacific plate and the overlapping layers of the North American plate. Local weaker sedimentary layers were forced at an angle and compressed into sandstone and shale.

Would you be surprised to know that Mount Diablo began rising relatively recently? It has been a topographical feature only for the past few million years. The 190-million-year-old rock in the central and highest peaks did not begin to rise until the Pliocene era about four million years ago. The erosion of the overlying rock exposed low-lying hills made of older igneous rock, which are now Mount Diablo's peaks. Major growth occurred during the late Pleistocene period, only 500,000 years ago. Forces associated with what is understood as a blind thrust fault beneath Mount Diablo creased the Franciscan Complex and the Great Valley layer. This pressure gave rise to a complex compressional fold.

Movements of all kinds have shaped the history of the mountain. The geological forces that gave rise to its unique location influenced the interactions of native life and newcomers, positioning Mount Diablo in a historical role in the development of the East San Francisco Bay Area.

PREHISTORIC LIFE AND EARLY INHABITANTS

Ancient remains preserved throughout the Mount Diablo State Park also chronicle the region's marine journey. Discoveries of fossilized clams, scallops, and oysters made in the sediment at the base of the mountain give some of the places near the Park their names, such as Shell Ridge. A rich mammal bone bed uncovered in a quarry at

Blackhawk provides evidence about the Park's prehistoric life. Sealed in stream deposits are incomplete skeletons of long-extinct mastodons, humpless camels, antelopes, three-toed and one-toed horses, as well as rhinos, saber-toothed cats, and short-faced dogs dating seven million years ago. (Dinosaurs did not roam with these beasts; Contra Costa County was under water during the Jurassic and Cretaceous periods).

Wild animals were not the only inhabitants of this area. Human skeletons found near the mountain indicate the arrival of the Indians about 5,000 years ago. The ethnographic territory of the Bay Miwok Indians encompassed Mount Diablo, making it home to a tribe of five subgroups in the area: the Scanlon, Chupcan, Julpan, Ompin, and Bolbon. The Bolbon tribelet (also known as the Volvon or Wolwon Indians) lived closest to Mount Diablo, crafting their homes among the sandstone formations on the south side of the peak and dwelling in structures framed with willow and thatched with tule and bunchgrass. Natives subsisted on worms, roots, nuts, acorns, and venison, and ventured to the higher elevations only to pray or perform ceremonies. Their primary village at the southeast base of the mountain became abandoned as the Bolbons were transported to Mission San José in 1805–1806. By the 1891 census, only four Indians remained alive, and the last died in 1900.

THE EVOLUTION OF MOUNT DIABLO'S NAME

Indian folklore reveres Contra Costa County's lone mountain. According to the Plains Miwok account of creation, Mol-luk (Condor-man) inhabited the north side of the peak. His wife, the rock on which he perched, gave birth to Wek-wek (Prairie falcon-man). Together Wek-wek and his grandfather, Coyote-man, created the native people and their land. In another tradition, at the Dawn of Time, water encompassed Mount Diablo and neighboring Reed's Peak. Creator Coyote and his assistant Eagleman fashioned the world and the native people from these islands. The natives referred to the mountain in other ways as well. The Costanoan Indians of West Contra Costa County originally named the peak "Kah Woo Koom," meaning "everywhere seen" and "laughing mountain."

The mountain's etymology altered course dramatically with the arrival of the Spanish. The first recorded sighting of Mount Diablo by European pioneers was by Lt. Don Pedro Fages in March 1772. Together with Father Juan Crespi, Fages conducted an expedition through the Carquinez Straits and along the western slope into the San Ramon Valley, later returning to hike the summit in 1772. Juan Bautista de Anza and Father Pedro Font explored the northern area of Mount Diablo between Pacheco and Concord, and Antioch and Byron, in 1776.

Tales of the interactions between the newcomers and the natives portray the evolution of the mountain's identity. Several accounts include a spiritual devil figure, hence the name "Diablo." The most widely accepted story is based on General Mariano Vallejo's April 16, 1850, report to the California State Legislature. An incident occurred in 1806 when Spanish troops, in pursuit of a band of Native Americans, decided to delay their capture until morning. The natives, stealing refuge in a thicket near Pacheco, escaped their pursuers in the middle of the night. Such a maneuver across the Carquinez Strait was only possible with the help of El Diablo, the Spaniards believed. Not long after did the thicket become known as "Monte de Diablo," something similar to what we hear today. Anglo settlers misinterpreted the term "monte" for "montaña" or "mountain," affixing the title to the most prominent landmark in the area. The Spanish word "monte" can mean either "mountain" or "thicket".

✣ ✣ ✣ ✣ ✣

MINING AND DEVELOPMENT

Mount Diablo played a pivotal role in regional economic development. Between the years 1850 and 1900, inland agricultural centers and water routes of the San Francisco Bay Area and of the Sacramento River Delta fueled the growth of Contra Costa County. Trips to Mount Diablo increased. In the 1870s, entrepreneurs constructed two horse carriage routes extending to within one mile of the summit, transforming the peak into a popular destination.

Mount Diablo's mineral resources drew even more people to the mountain during the latter half of the nineteenth century. After its discovery in 1859, coal was mined, with brief interruptions, until 1902 in Nortonville and Somersville, stimulating growth in Clayton, Concord, Martinez, and Pittsburg. Coal fueled railroads and river steamers and supplied energy throughout the Bay Area. Over four million tons were mined over a fifty-year period, with production reaching its zenith in the 1880s.

Excavations of other minerals were performed as well. A copper rush occurred between 1862 and 1864, giving rise to a small-scale mining operation on the northwest side of Mount Diablo. Production totaled approximately 40,000 pounds. Gold and silver were found in the copper ores, but no significant quantities were extracted. A major quicksilver district was established in 1863 along the northeast base of Mount Diablo, and mercury was produced for the next century. Mines yielded 12,300 flasks of mercury, an amount valued at $1.5 million. In the early years, mercury was in high demand because it provided a means to extract gold from the Sierra Nevada. It was also vital to the U.S. government during World Wars I and II.

By 1900, the population in Contra Costa County had reached 18,000. After the quarries closed, some miners transitioned to ranching. Abandoned mining buildings became barns, railroad ties were flipped vertically for fence posts, and boilers were converted to water troughs. Ranches sprang up across Mount Diablo. Port and Navy operations expanded rapidly over the next several decades.

Preservation of Mount Diablo began on June 19, 1921, with the acquisition of 630 acres by the State of California. Neighboring East Bay Regional Park District was founded in 1934. The completion of the Bay Bridge in 1936 created additional demand for housing in the East Bay; however, the Oakland and Berkeley hills barred inland movement until the Caldecott Tunnel was constructed in 1937. The improvement of roads and freeways allowed the inland valleys to develop into suburban communities of the Bay Area during post-War economic expansion. Residents soon became emotionally tethered to Mount Diablo. With the population and housing boom in Contra Costa County (approaching one million people), the public and their political representatives saw an urgent need to protect open space. Communities approved funding for the expansion of Mount Diablo State Park, which now covers 20,000 acres.

THE STATE PARK

Mount Diablo is an extraordinary landmark. Its focal point scrapes 3,849 feet, endowing visitors with legendary views and permitting sight of the Sierra Nevada mountain range on clear-weather days. Situated at the peak is a magnificent native-stone building, housing a museum and visitor center designed to help Park visitors visualize and appreciate the natural and cultural history of Mount Diablo. Built by skilled craftsmen from the Civilian Conservation Corps (CCC), this structure has quite a history of its own. On October 22, 1938, men from the CCC, all former World War I veterans, arrived at Mount Diablo State Park. CCC Company 2932-V was assigned to CCC Camp Mount Diablo (SP-9). The majority of the enrollees formerly had served at Mount Diablo State Park on two different occasions—October 23, 1934, to June 10, 1935, and October 23, 1935, to May 10, 1936.

The building was erected in accordance with specifications prepared by architects and engineers of the National Park Service and the California Division of Beaches and Parks (Department of Parks and Recreation). All work was accomplished under the administration of the National Park Service and under the day-to-day management and supervision of the California Department of Beaches and Parks, while the in-camp management and supervision of the enrollees rested with the U.S. Army.

The assignments of each of the CCC men depended upon their skills. Men in the best physical condition were appointed to the Park's rock quarry on Fossil Ridge and were served by drivers who trucked the loads to the top. Crews at the summit constructed foundation forms, performing the arduous tasks of concrete spreading, mortar application, and fitting of the stone masonry. Workers relocated the famous Standard Diablo Beacon Light to the apex of the building, positioning it as a location beam for airplanes. It was moved from its perch atop a 75-foot steel tower where it had been situated originally on April 15, 1928. At the time of relocation, the beacon was subject to the jurisdiction of the State of California, having been transferred from Standard Oil (now Chevron) ownership on January 1, 1939. With the work completed, the CCC workers departed Mount Diablo on August 15, 1941, establishing a magnificent legacy of the Civilian Conservation Corps for the people of Contra Costa County, the State of California, and the United States. Mount Diablo State Park was designated a "National Natural Landmark" by the National Park Service in 1982.

A PEAK STILL RISING

A climb to the summit immerses visitors in Mount Diablo's history. Hikers rising to the top are invited to hear stories of how the mountain itself has risen. And it is true that the peak continues to ascend, albeit very gradually. Though the forces of subduction and erosion may keep the elevation from changing significantly for thousands of years, the ancient stresses that folded and lifted the mountain continue to elevate it approximately one inch every 100 years.

The pages of *Mountain Lore* hold the stories of small treasures tucked throughout Mount Diablo. An estimated 250 creeks, canyons, trails, springs, and locations exist within the over 20,000 acres of Mount Diablo State Park. Most of these locations are identified by a place name, which depicts common fauna, flora, topography, or local historical significance. *Mountain Lore* concentrates on 101 of these obscure place names. Among the place names are a few unusual words, but most originate from people who have had a historic presence on Mount Diablo. Some of these place names originated before the establishment of the Park (1921) and were designated by settlers in the mid-to-late 1800s and early 1900s. Many decades have passed since the creation of many of these names, causing them to become esoteric or lost. *Mountain Lore* endeavors to revitalize the origins and significance of these place names.

The following 101 place names can be found on the *Trail Map Of Mount Diablo State Park*, Sixth Edition, published by the Mount Diablo Interpretive Association. The letters and numbers in parentheses following the place name refer to the map's grid coordinates for the location in the Park. Signposts marked with place names correspond with most of the trails and locations in the Park. Together, these unique narratives illustrate the colorful history of Mount Diablo.

WIND CAVES AT ROCK CITY ROI PEERS

Place Names of Mount Diablo

ALAMO CREEK
(S20)

The word "Alamo" is Spanish for "poplar." It was given to the town, and eventually to the creek, because poplar trees once grew abundantly in the valley and along the streams. The poplar tree in this area is named the Fremont cottonwood *(Populus fremontii)*. This tree was named after John C. Fremont, the American military officer, surveyor, and first Republican Party candidate for the office of President of the United States, who discovered the species with American frontiersman Kit Carson, near Pyramid Lake, Nevada, in 1844.

CHARLES WEBBER ©1999 CALIFORNIA ACADEMY OF SCIENCES

POPLAR TREE • *Populus fremontii*

ALDER CREEK
(P15)

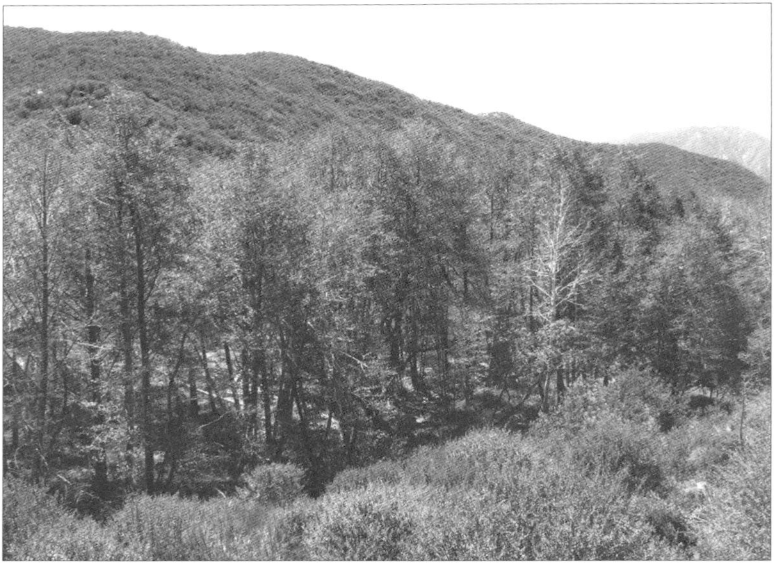

ALDER TREES • *Alnus rhombifolia*

© 2008 GARY A. MONROE
BON TERRA CONSULTING

Named for the white alder trees *(Alnus rhombifolia)* that abound along streams, as in the above photograph. These trees thrive throughout the Park, especially where water flows year-round.

AMPHITHEATER TRAIL
(T18)

SANDSTONE FORMATIONS NEAR AMPHITHEATER TRAIL MIKE WOODRING

Webster's Dictionary defines "amphitheater" (also spelled "amphitheatre") as "a level place surrounded by rising ground." This accurately describes the setting on Amphitheater Trail, one quarter of a mile east of Old Finley Road where you will cross a small flat valley surrounded by vertical sandstone cliffs and rocks.

ANGEL KERLEY ROAD
(L14)

ANGEL KERLEY RIDING HER HORSE IN THE PARK KIM BRUMLEVE

The fire road is named for Angelina E. Toscani Kerley (1908–1987), who owned and operated the Diablo Ranch on North Gate Road on the western slope of Mount Diablo. Angel took control of the 300-head, 2,000+-acre, working cattle ranch in 1958 as part of a divorce settlement from her husband.

Angel was born in Santa Rosa, California, and graduated from college with a major in English. She married

Robert D. Kerley in 1934, and settled with him in Berkeley. Her husband operated Allied Automatic, a vending machine company in Oakland. Angel was an accomplished horse rider, successfully competing in 100-mile rides in 24-hour periods.

In 1980, Angel sold 1,869 acres of Diablo Ranch to the State of California for $3.3 million. She donated 281 acres to the California State Parks Foundation in 1980 for tax credits, land which was then purchased by the State of California seven years later for $87,000. Angel had two children: Robert Kerley, Jr., and Joan Kerley Brumleve. Joan died in 2000. Tom Brumleve, Joan's husband, currently lives on a 61-acre in-holding ranch on Mount Diablo.

ARROYO DEL CERRO
(112)

ARROYO DEL CERRO RANCH MIKE WOODRING

Spanish for "hillside creek."

ARROYO PICNIC AREA
(N17)

ARROYO PICNIC AREA RICH MCDREW

"Arroyo" is a Spanish word meaning "stream," "brook," "creek," or "gully."

BALANCING ROCK
(P17)

BALANCING ROCK MIKE WOODRING

Along Knobcone Point Road about one mile east of Curry Point, this massive eroded sandstone rock balances precariously above and along the road. An exact replica of this rock is on public display inside the Lindsay Wildlife Museum at 1931 First Avenue, Walnut Creek.

BBQ TERRACE HORSE & GROUP CAMP (M15)

BARBECUE TERRACE PHOTO COURTESY OF BOB COOPER

This equestrian and group camp and nearby BBQ (Barbecue) Terrace Road were so named because the camp is situated on a plateau with a large natural-rock barbecue grill. The large size of the grill lends itself to cooking for many people.

BICENTENNIAL TREE
(L9)

BICENTENNIAL TREE RACHEL HAISLET

In 1987, the Acalanes Chapter of the Daughters of the American Revolution (DAR) approached Park management with the idea to observe the 200th anniversary of the creation of the Constitution of the United States by dedicating a tree. A coast live oak tree *(Quercus agrifolia)* was selected about one quarter of a mile south from the parking lot along the Mitchell Canyon [fire] Road. A trail signpost identifies this tree. This tree was selected because 200 years before 1987, it was just an acorn about to give birth to a magnificent living organism just as the Constitution was giving life to a struggling neophyte nation in the summer of 1787.

BLACK HAWK RIDGE ROAD
(P18)

The name Black Hawk Ridge Road shares history with nearby Blackhawk Ranch. When residing on a ranch (bought in 1857) on the San Francisco Peninsula with his wife Adeline Mills, Ansel Ives Easton purchased an Irish-born stallion called Black Hawk. When the couple moved to the East Bay in 1917, they named their new ranch after the horse.

The stallion, allegedly the first thoroughbred transported to California for racing and breeding, was named after Indian warrior Black Hawk. Leader of the northern Illinois Sauk (Sac) and Fox Indian tribes, Black Hawk became famous for his role in the 1832 wars opposing President Andrew Jackson's policy of relocating Native Americans west of the Mississippi River.

CHIEF BLACK HAWK, CIRCA 1837
MCKENNEY-HALL COLLECTION, STATE HISTORICAL SOCIETY OF IOWA, IOWA CITY

BLACK SAGE ROAD
(N19)

BLACK SAGE • *Salvia mellifera*

Black sage *(Salvia mellifera),* also known as the honey sage, is a California native evergreen shrub prolific in dry, rocky environments throughout the Park. As members of the mint family, sages have potent aromatic foliage. Its whorls of white, purplish flowers entice hummingbirds, bees, and butterflies.

BLAISDELL TRAIL
(R10)

BLAISDELL TRAIL MIKE WOODRING

The trail is named for Harry Lee Blaisdell (1890–1964), superintendent of the Central Coast Division of the State Parks and first "warden" of Mount Diablo State Park in the 1920s. Harry was a native of Massachusetts.

BOBS POND
(R17)

This man-made stock pond below Windy Point along Tassajara Creek Trail was named for Robert "Bob" Gemmell Adams (1925–1999). In 1998, when Bob was a Director on Save Mount Diablo's (SMD) Board, SMD purchased the 427-acre Silva cattle ranch for $750,000. Bob personally donated $25,000 to help secure the ranch's acquisition. SMD decided to honor Bob with the naming of the pond shortly before his untimely July 21st death. In 2003, SMD transferred the property to the State of California to be included in Mount Diablo State Park. The July 25, 1999, obituary in the *Contra Costa Times* states the following:

JEANNE THOMAS
ROBERT "BOB" GEMMELL ADAMS

A third generation Californian, Bob was born in Oakland in 1925. He graduated from the University of California at Berkeley, and the Boalt Hall School of Law. His legal career took him to post World War II Germany as a civilian attached to the U.S. Army, and to a position in Sacramento with the California State Board of Equalization before he entered private practice in Oakland until his retirement in 1987.

BRIONES–MOUNT DIABLO REGIONAL TRAIL
(115)

BRIONES—MOUNT DIABLO REGIONAL TRAIL AT MACEDO RANCH

This trail extends from Briones Regional Park through the Diablo Foothills Regional Park to Mount Diablo. It is named for the prosperous farmer Ramon Briones (1814–1875). Briones Valley was also named after him. In 1844, Ramon married Louise Moraga Briones (1816–1906). Initially residing in San Pablo and Pinole, the couple moved to Oakland in 1869. They had seven children. Ramon was killed in a railroad accident.

BRUCE LEE ROAD
(M9)

BRUCE LEE APPLIANCES WALNUT CREEK STOREFRONT, 1950s

Bruce Royal Lee (1916–1985) was President of the Concord/Mount Diablo Trail Ride Association, founded in 1941 by avid horse lovers who enjoyed riding in the hills of Contra Costa County. Beginning with 18 riders, they incorporated in 1945 and purchased 200 acres on the north side of Mount Diablo in 1960. Today, about 100 families are members of the Association. Bruce was a dedicated and tireless advocate for building and improving riding and hiking trails in and around Mount Diablo State Park. He was the owner/operator of Bruce Lee Appliances in Walnut Creek. He and his wife, Bobbie M. Lee, and son Marty and daughter Deborah, lived in Pleasant Hill.

BUCKEYE TRAIL
(K14)

CALIFORNIA BUCKEYE • *Aesculus californica*

ROBERT POTTS
© 2007 CALIFORNIA
ACADEMY OF SCIENCES

Named for the California buckeye trees *(Aesculus californica)* that are not only common along this trail but throughout the Park. This tree drops its leaves by midsummer, earlier than other deciduous trees, as a mechanism to prevent stress during dry conditions. Its fragrant flowers and large, poisonous buckeye balls appear in autumn.

BURMA ROAD
(K13)

J. FRANK VALLE RIESTRA

BURMA ROAD, EDITH VALLE RIESTRA PICTURED

This Diablo Ranch road was named in the 1960's by Angel Kerley (see "Angel Kerley Road," page 16) after the original Burma Road. The construction of the original road began in 1937 to bring supplies through the Southeast Asian country of Burma (now Myanmar) to beleaguered China to help them resist the Japanese invasion. The actual 717-mile Burma Road was mostly built by the Chinese. One hundred sixty thousand workers hacked the mountain road with virtually no mechanized equipment. Even though Angel's nearly 5-mile Burma Road was not of the same scale as the original, the challenging engineering feat through the steep terrain of Mount Diablo was reminiscent of the Burmese Himalayas.

CAMEL ROCK TRAIL
(J13)

CAMEL ROCK MIKE WOODRING

This route is named for a camel-shaped rock structure situated 1.6 miles up trail. The formation is one of the visible remains of ancient geological movements. The ridge across the valley beyond Camel Rock comprises lower Eocene age sandstones and shale, while the basin west of the Mount Diablo Thrust Fault possesses Cretaceous Period characteristics. Both components represent forces that began to elevate Mount Diablo four million years ago.

CARDINET OAKS ROAD
(O11)

CONTRA COSTA TIMES

GEORGE CARDINET OF BACK CREEK TRAIL AND CARDINET OAKS ROAD

Named for George H. Cardinet, Jr. (1909–2007), the former President of the Cardinet Candy Company, a business started by his father. George was a President of the Concord/Mount Diablo Trail Ride Association and founder of the California Horseman's Association. Known as "the father of California's trail system," he helped to establish many of the hiking and riding trails in Mount Diablo State Park over the past 70 years. Another trail, the George Cardinet/Back Creek Trail, was dedicated in his honor in 1992. His wife Margaret died in 1992. They raised four children.

CASTLE ROCK TRAIL
(114)

CASTLE ROCK MIKE WOODRING

The origin of this place name announces itself to hikers trekking one-plus mile into Pine Canyon from the East Bay Regional Park District's Castle Rock Regional Recreation Area. A magnificent rock towers in the east casting its shadow upon "Little Yosemite," reaching an elevation of 972 feet. Peregrine falcons, golden eagles, and red-tailed hawks nest among its extraordinary sandstone formations.

CHARLES POND
(S17)

CHARLES POND MIKE WOODRING

This man-made stock pond is at a secluded location a short distance east of Tassajara Creek Trail. It was named by Save Mount Diablo (SMD) for Charles Phillip Gresham (1917–), who, with his brother Walter, generously donated $100,000 in 1999 to help SMD secure the acquisition of the 427-acre Silva cattle ranch. In 2003, SMD transferred the property to the State of California to be included in Mount Diablo State Park.

Born in Oklahoma, Charles moved to Southern California with his family as a teenager. In the Summer 2003 Edition of *Diablo Watch,* SMD wrote of Charles:

"He describes himself as a little bit of a hippie—he wandered the railroads during the Depression, working odd jobs and then on a ranch in New Mexico. Both fit in well with his love of hiking. Later he studied art, but took a job in a warehouse because he liked physical work. Sydney Engelberg was his partner of 50 years and an accomplished painter and commercial artist for magazines, including the **New Yorker***. Eventually they settled in a tiny twelve foot wide house on San Francisco's Telegraph Hill. When Sydney became ill, Charles took care of him for ten years, rarely leaving the house. Sydney died in September 1997 and Charles decided he wanted to get out, hike and help preserve land."*

CHASE POND
(O15)

CHASE POND

MIKE WOODRING

Robert Noble Burgess (1878–1965) named this remote, bucolic pond in memory of his maternal grandmother, Hanna Burgess, nee Chase (1801–1887). In the early 1900s, Robert Noble Burgess was the foremost real estate developer and land speculator in Contra Costa and neighboring counties. As an entrepreneur businessman and raconteur, he bought and sold hundreds of thousands of acres over a 20-year period. He purchased the 10,000-acre Oakwood Park Stock Farm in 1913 from the niece of Dan Cook, Louise Boyd, nee Arner (1887–1972) (see "Dan Cook Canyon" place name), and initiated the upscale community of Diablo. Chase Pond and the nearby Mountain Springs Creek are five miles as a crow flies up Mount Diablo to the northeast, but has a nexus to the community of Diablo and its early water source. Beginning in 1895, the water to this area was gravity-fed to Diablo from Mountain Springs Creek using a 6-inch cast iron pipe.

Robert Noble Burgess was born in St. John, New Brunswick, Canada, and was one of nine children of Joshua Chase Burgess (1842–1935), a Presbyterian pastor, and Mary Helen Burgess, nee Noble (1850–1920). Mary's mother, Hanna, is the origin of the "Chase" in Chase Pond and Chase Pond Road. Robert married Anne Holcomb Webster Burgess, nee Fish (1886–1953), on July 20, 1909, in Berkeley, CA. Anne called him "Robb." They had five children—Fanny, Suzanne, Nancy, Polly, and Robin—and 16 grandchildren.

Louise Boyd was a famous woman and Bay Area philanthropist who once owned a large part of what is now Mount Diablo State Park. She was born in San Rafael and died in San Francisco. She came from a very wealthy family, her grandfather having made a fortune in the California Gold Rush. She inherited the family fortune at the age of 13 in 1920, and succeeded her father as President of the Boyd Investment Company. She financed and led several expeditions to the Arctic. She became an expert on the fiords and glaciers on the east coast of Greenland. She became the first woman to fly over the North Pole at the age of 68.

CHASE POND WAS INCORRECTLY IDENTIFIED AS BEING NAMED AFTER SAMUEL CHASE IN THE ORIGINAL *51 UNCOMMON PLACE NAMES OF MOUNT DIABLO STATE PARK*.

CHINA WALL
(115)

CHINA WALL MIKE WOODRING

Located north of Macedo Ranch stretches a ridge of rocks. This is a terminally eroded layer of sandstone, thrust into vertical position by the mountain's piercement. Its apparent likeness, albeit miniature, to the Great Wall of China gives it this name.

CIVILIAN CONSERVATION CORPS TRAIL (M17)

POOL AT ROCK CITY NEAR THIS TRAIL CARL NIELSON

The acronym "CCC" stands for the Civilian Conservation Corps, founded in 1933 by the Federal government in order to plant trees, combat fires and tree diseases, and otherwise add to the value of the forest domain. The CCC was disbanded during World War II after serving the purpose of training and educating youth throughout the country during times of high unemployment. It was an

instrument for preventing delinquency and providing opportunities for young men to learn a profession. The CCC was responsible for many unique and useful work projects in Mount Diablo State Park, only one of seven California State Parks to benefit from CCC labor.

In addition to the CCC Trail, a 200-man company, all veterans of World War I, built the Summit Visitor Center from quarried stone extracted only six miles away near Rock City. The veterans also built camping and picnic sites, including parking spaces, a water supply and distribution system, restrooms, stone fireplaces, hewn tables and benches, culverts, retaining walls. They also constructed many access roads and trails.

CLAYTON OAKS ROAD
(O10)

Joel Henry Clayton (1812–1872) was born in England, the eldest of 12 children. Immigrating to America in 1837, he ventured to California, becoming a true pioneer of the early West. A talented mining engineer, prospector, trader, farmer, community developer, and all around entrepreneur, his legendary activities across the country and along the entire West Coast earned him much respect and are recorded in many places. Joel first saw Clayton Valley in 1843. In 1853, he purchased land, and in l856, recorded and began developing his new town of Clayton. Unfortunately, he died of "quick pneumonia" after exposure in a chilling storm. He had struggled home carrying a sick calf that was dead by the time he reached the farmhouse. Joel and his wife, Margaret Ellen McLay Clayton (1820–1908), are buried in Clayton's Live Oak Cemetery. Four of their nine children survived them.

RACHEL HAISLET

ENTRANCE TO THE TOWN OF CLAYTON

COFFEEBERRY SPRING
(K13)

COFFEEBERRY PLANT • *Rhamnus californica* © 2002 LYNN WATSON

The coffeeberry *(Rhamnus californica)* is an evergreen shrub native to California, growing near streams and springs throughout the Park. Birds and mammals enjoy its berry (inedible to humans), which resembles but is unrelated to the berry that produces coffee.

COULTER PINE TRAIL
(M9)

RICHARD B. LEWIS III © 2009 BON TERRA CONSULTING

COULTER PINE • *Pinus coulteri*

The Coulter pine *(Pinus coulteri)*, also named big cone pine, bull pine, and pitch pine, is one of three California native pines that flourish in the Park. The other two are the knobcone pine *(Pinus attenuata)* and gray pine *(Pinus sabiniana)*. The species, found in the cooler Park environments (north shaded slopes), was named after Thomas Coulter, an Irish botanist and physician. These pines produce huge pine cones—up to one foot long and weighing five pounds! Many years ago indigenous people enjoyed the pine nuts tucked inside the pine cones.

CRESTED JAY ROAD
(R11)

CRESTED JAY • *Cyanocitta stelleri* © 2008 GARY MCDONALD

This gravel ranch road is named for the Steller's jay *(Cyanocitta stelleri)*, a bird discovered in 1741 by German naturalist Georg Wilhelm Steller. Also known as the long-crested jay, the mountain jay, and the pine jay, it is the sole crested jay west of the Rocky Mountains. Its diet comprises two-thirds plant matter and one-third animal matter. It can be spotted throughout the Park, but sightings are mostly likely among the lower elevation coniferous forests, particularly in the Three Springs area.

CURRY CANYON ROAD
(O17)

CURRY CANYON INDIAN GRINDING HOLES

RACHEL HAISLET

James R. Curry (1835–1908), a native of Virginia, and his wife, Ellen Callan Curry, a native of London, England, were early pioneers in Contra Costa County, settling in the Clayton area in 1858. James was engaged in the livery business and established the first stage line between Clayton and Oakland, and another one to Nortonville, in the Black Diamond coal-mining region. He made two trips back to his Virginian home utilizing a team of oxen. The Currys had eight children, seven of whom were boys.

CURRY CAVE ROAD
(Q16)

CAVE AT CAVE POINT (RICH MCDREW, PICTURED) BURT BOGARDUS

This dirt ranch road was named in memory of the Curry family (see the "Curry Canyon Road" place name). "Cave" was added because this road is between Cave Point and Curry Canyon Road. Small sandstone caves surround Cave Point. Cave Point and much of Curry Cave Road are private property, owned by the Ettore S. Bertagnolli family.

DAN COOK CANYON
(L16)

FOOT BRIDGE IN DAN COOK CANYON

Daniel Cook was the owner of a 6,000-acre ranch on the southwestern slopes of Mount Diablo. The property was first purchased by the famous Southern Pacific Railroad's "Big Four," Charles Crocker, Mark Hopkins, Collis Huntington, and Leland Stanford, giving it the name "Railroad Ranch" (1877–1880). It was managed, and subsequently owned, by another Southern Pacific Rail magnate, David Colton. Dan and his wife, Caroline

Colton Cook, inherited the ranch after Caroline's father's death on October 10, 1878, due to a horse-riding accident. It became the "Cook Ranch" (1880-1889). By 1881, Dan and Caroline and their young son had died, and Dan's brother Seth Cook (1830–1889) took over the ranch. After Seth's death in 1889, the ranch was left to Cook's niece and was henceforth known as "Oakwood Park Stock Farm" (1890–1912). Ranch operation relied on raising thoroughbred horses.

The original ranchland included Dan Cook Canyon, Rock City, Devils Slide, and central portions of the Park along what is now South Gate Road. The Diablo Country Club stands on the site of the old headquarters of the Railroad Ranch/Cook Ranch/Oakwood Park Stock Farm.

DENNING COMPASS

(O13)

On the observation deck of the Summit Museum sits a glass-enclosed octagonal rotunda or cupola that contains a masonry pedestal. Atop the pedestal is a bronze compass aligned to TRUE north, with the following inscription:

PLACED IN MEMORY OF
FRANCES JEAN DENNING
LT. COL. NORMAN EDWIN
DENNING, USMC

RICH MCDREW

DENNING COMPASS

Park visitors have inquired about the origin of the Denning Compass. Norman Edwin Denning (1911–1983) and his wife Frances Jean [nee Warner] Denning (1913–1984) were frequent visitors to Mount Diablo State Park. They were avid Park equestrians who lived in the nearby town of Diablo. Norman and Frances were married in Florida in 1940, and had four children. Norman was a highly decorated Marine Corps officer and aviator. Frances' great uncle, Thorburn "James" Cumberpatch, who was also an aviator, purportedly played a role in establishing the Standard Oil aviator

navigation beacon on top of Mount Diablo in 1928. It was because of their family's involvement and love of Mount Diablo that the Denning children, upon the death of their parents, wanted to give a gift to the Park in memory of their parents. They wanted to do something that their parents would approve of and that would add to the public's experience in the Park.

In 1985 and 1986, several ideas were discussed with Park superintendent William Beat, Supervising Park Ranger Richard Gililland, and Park Ranger Mary Angle. The bronze compass was agreed upon because of the family's involvement with aviation and the beacon. The very talented Park stone mason, Don Biaggi, cemented local native stone around the already existing plain cement pedestal. Affixed atop the pedestal was the cast bronze compass. This replaced a metal lid that, when removed, revealed the copper bolt survey mark placed by government surveyor Leander Ransom in 1851. The work on the Denning Compass was completed on January 16, 1997. It is interesting to note that the ashes of Norman and Frances were scattered on Mount Diablo.

DONNER CABIN
(N10)

DONNER CABIN CIRCA 1980 ROBERT E. DOYLE

A popular trailhead on the north side of Mount Diablo State Park is called "Regency Gate." Regency Gate is at the end of Regency Drive in Clayton. This trailhead is one of the best routes to access Donner Canyon and to find the Donner Cabin site. It is a no-fee Park hike entrance, but there are no restrooms or potable water.

The beautiful Donner Canyon was named for John Donner and his descendants. He was not a member of the ill-fated Donner Party that attempted to cross the Sierra Nevada Mountains in a horrific snowstorm in the

1840s. According to the 1880 census in Clayton, John Donner was born in 1814 in Canada and was employed as a farmer. His parents were born in Germany. John and his family cultivated a farm in the area of Donner Canyon in the 1870s.

Two miles south of Regency Gate on the level Donner Canyon fire-road, there existed in the 1930s a 160-acre parcel leased by a hunting club. Members of the club built a two-bedroom house on a massive concrete foundation overlooking Donner Creek. The house had such a large fireplace that a grown person could actually stand up in it! The house was appropriately called the "Donner Cabin."

On May 11, 1951, William Alford Hetherington (1906–1983) and his wife, Blenda Hetherington (1901–1995), purchased the 160 acres from Janet Knight. William was a native Californian and a professor at the University of California, Berkeley. The Donner Cabin and acreage were primarily used by the Hetheringtons as a summer retreat. The Hetheringtons sold this parcel in 1973 to the California State Park system. They were eager to sell their property to the State because it was their desire to have their property put into a permanent protection status. From 1976 to 1980, Robert (Bob) E. Doyle lived in the Donner Cabin as a bachelor while attending college and working as a ranger for the East Bay Regional Park District's

DONNER CABIN CIRCA 1980

ROBERT E. DOYLE

(EBRPD) Black Diamond Preserve. Bob paid the State of California a rental fee, but more importantly, he was a caretaker/protector for the Donner Cabin. Bob is currently the EBRPD's General Manager headquartered in Oakland, CA. Bob reminisced recently about how the Donner Cabin and nearby barn miraculously survived the devastating 1977 wildfire on Mount Diablo. This fire burned the entire northern portion of Mount Diablo State Park from the summit to the bottom of Donner Canyon. Ironically, the Donner Cabin was destroyed by an arson fire on New Year's Eve of 1982.

Today, Park visitors can still see remnants of the Donner Cabin's concrete foundation. The cabin's location is across the Donner Canyon fire road from the foot of Donner Cabin Trail.

DONNER CANYON
(N10)

DONNER CREEK RACHEL HAISLET

This beautiful canyon on Mount Diablo's north side is named for John Donner and his descendants. According to the 1880 census in Clayton, John was born in 1814 in Canada and was employed as a farmer. His father and mother were born in Germany. He was not a member of the ill-fated Donner Party that came to California in the 1840s.

DUNN CREEK
(S11)

DUNN CREEK RICH MCDREW

Dunn Creek flows from the eastern slopes of Mount Diablo in the Three Springs area and eventually empties into the larger Marsh Creek. The entire length of Dunn Creek is within the boundaries of Mount Diablo State Park. Much of the lower, flatter sections of the creek flow adjacent to Olympia Trail. It was in this area that on November 11, 1891, Mary E. Dunn (1853–1927), a resident of Oakland (living at 1612 Myrtle Street), purchased 40 acres for $400 from William and Julia Martindale. Dunn Creek passed through the middle of her property. On August 26, 1898, Mary sold the property to her eldest son, William L. Dunn, for $1,000.

It was Mary who named this creek in memory of her deceased husband, Patrick Dunn (1840–1906). The couple immigrated to America from Ireland in 1855 and settled in Oakland. All four of their children were born in California: William L. Dunn (1876–1971), Thomas F. Dunn (1878–1965), Mary J. Dunn (1882–1975), and John J. Dunn (1883–1964).

EMMONS CANYON

(K16)

EMMONS CANYON MIKE WOODRING

The name "Emmons Canyon" is connected to the historical Emmons family farm in the Green Valley area dating back to the 1920s. The farm and a lovely Victorian home were situated at the mouth of the canyon in the flatter foothill and valley sections. George Wellington Emmons (1859–1928), a wealthy entrepreneur, owned and operated a 640-acre farm from approximately 1919 until his death on October 9, 1928. The farm was an avocation for Emmons, as his primary business was Emmons Storage and Drayage Company, in Alameda, California. The

main family home for him and wife Harriet A. Emmons (1871–1923) and their three daughters (Gertrude, Gladys, and Marjorie) was also in Alameda. The farm employed 12 people and raised cattle, pigs, goats, and sheep.

George was a native of the Bay Area, as were his two sisters, Idella (1855–1949) and Mabel (1866–1936). It is believed that George acquired his farm—a section or 1/36th of a township—in a bankruptcy settlement in 1919. Several years earlier, George purchased shares in the Mount Diablo Park Company (MDPC), a business created by real estate developer Robert Noble Burgess. Burgess' company encompassed more than 15,000 acres on the western slopes of Mount Diablo. He envisioned grandiose plans for an affluent community of 10,000 people. In 1913, the shareholders elected George Emmons to be the MDPC general manager of all ranching operations.

FALCON ROAD
(113)

PEREGRINE FALCON • *Falco peregrinus* © 2009 RON WOLF

Named for the indigenous peregrine falcon *(Falco peregrinus)* that was reintroduced into the nearby Castle Rock (see "Castle Rock Trail" place name) in 1989. Peregrine is derived from the Latin word for "wanderer." The species, nearly wiped out from the pesticide DDT (banned in 1972), has recovered due to environmental regulations, federal protection (1973 Endangered Species Act), and the cooperative work of government agencies, conservation organizations, and volunteers. The peregrine falcon can dive at speeds exceeding 200 miles per hour, making it the fastest animal on earth! This crow-sized raptor is distinguished by its short tail, pointed wings, dark cap, and dark cheek ("mustache") marks below the eyes.

FELT SPRING
(Q14)

FELT SPRING — RICH MCDREW

William Felt named the spring in memory of his wife, Matilda Felt (1860–1906). Both were natives of Sweden. William was a miner in Colorado and a railroad man in San Francisco before purchasing 160 acres on the east side of Mount Diablo in 1905 from C.H. Bradley. The *Contra Costa Gazette* reported that William "made a little clearing and built a little house for himself and wife." On September 29, 1906, Matilda unexpectedly died of heart failure on the "slopes of Mount Diablo" at the age of 46. She was fluent in seven languages and was governess for several affluent families.

Felt Spring is located off-road in Rhine Canyon.

FROG POND
(P15)

FROG POND MIKE WOODRING

This man-made stock pond sits at the end of Frog Pond Road at an elevation of 1,539 feet. Frog Pond is fed by winter rains and a year-round spring. Some water is always present at the pond, and thus has attracted the Sierran Treefrog *(Pseudacris sierra)*, also called the Pacific Chorus Frog.

GIBRALTAR ROCK
(N17)

UPPER PORTION OF GIBRALTAR ROCK ALONG SOUTH GATE ROAD RICH MCDREW

The "Rock of Gibraltar" is an imposing natural rock formation near the southern tip of Spain in the strait between Europe and Africa at the entrance to the Mediterranean Sea. Similarly, Gibraltar Rock in Mount Diablo State Park marks the natural gateway to Rock City along South Gate Road.

GLOBE LILY TRAIL

(L10)

GLOBE LILY • *Calochortus pulchellus* © 2008 GARY A. MOMROE

Named for the Mount Diablo fairy lantern *(Calochortus pulchellus)*, also known as the globe lily and globe tulip, which is particularly prevalent in the area of this trail in the springtime. The *C. pulchellus* is a California native plant and is only found on Mount Diablo. It is included in the California Native Plant Society's inventory of rare and endangered plants. The look-alike *Calochortus albus* (white globe tulip) is found in other parts of the Bay Area and California.

GOVERNMENT ROAD
(K13)

GOVERNMENT ROAD SIGNPOST MIKE WOODRING

In 1851, two U.S. Army officers, Majors Robert Allen and Robert Loring, purchased a 3,000-acre ranch on the western slope of Mount Diablo. Their property was appropriately called "Government Ranch." Government Road was within their property.

GREEN RANCH ROAD
(O14)

GREEN RANCH

PHOTOGRAPH BY ROGER STURTEVANT
WILLIAM W. WURSTER / WBE COLLECTION
ENVIRONMENTAL DESIGN ARCHIVES,
UNIVERSITY OF CALIFORNIA, BERKELEY

This fire road is named for "Greenhill Ranch," property of Berkeley residents Robert Clarke Green (1905–1981) and his wife Deborah Bixby Green (1904–1959). In 1938, they built a summer/country house on their south-facing, 170-acre parcel near Mount Diablo's summit. Renowned architect William Wurster designed the house. The summer estate included a large swimming pool, tennis court,

and guest quarters. The State of California acquired the property in 1965. The house was demolished in 1993. In 1995, one of the Greens' daughters, Deborah Green Seymour, wrote the following: "We all called it 'Diablo.' It was also known as the 'Green Ranch,' although officially its title was 'Greenhill Ranch.' We learned a lot at Diablo. What we gained from our parents and the rangers was a love and respect for the mountain and its inhabitants, and the responsibility for taking care of this special place."

GRIZZLY BEAR ROAD
(Q17)

GRIZZLY BEAR • *Ursus arctos californicus*

GERALD AND BUFF CORSI

The California grizzly bear *(Ursus arctos californicus)* inhabited Mount Diablo before man began to settle the land in and around the mountain. These bears were hunted to extinction by the early 1900s. The California grizzly, named the official state animal in 1953, is stamped on the California state flag. Sports teams, such as the California Golden Bears of the University of California, Berkeley, also allude to the grizzly.

HETHERINGTON TRAIL
(N10)

Named for William Alford Hetherington (1906–1983) and wife Blenda Hetherington. His parents were Clark Wilson Hetherington and Daisy Alford Hetherington.

RACHEL HAISLET

HETHERINGTON TRAIL

William was a native Californian and a professor at the University of California, Berkeley. He died in San Francisco and was buried in Tulare, California. William and Blenda owned a 160-acre parcel in Donner Canyon beginning in 1951. The State Park System acquired this parcel in 1973. The Hetheringtons insisted on selling their property to the State because it was their desire that the property be put into permanent protection status. Blenda wrote the following in a 1973 letter: "We are gratified that 23 years of protection and a policy of 'bringing to' rather than 'taking from' the area have helped reclaim certain vulnerable areas and allowed normal growth in others. We feel certain that we left the land better than we found it and hope the area can still be given some protection from overcrowding and devastating practices."

HIDDEN POND
(O15)

HIDDEN POND — MIKE WOODRING

This man-made stock pond was named due to its relatively inaccessible location in the Park. It fills up with rain water in the winter, but becomes bone dry by late summer. Hidden Pond is located a quarter mile uphill and north of Frog Pond Road.

JACKASS CANYON
(S19)

JACKASS CANYON RICH MCDREW

"Jackass" is a colloquial word for male donkey. It is also an unflattering nickname occasionally given to a person who is extremely foolish or intractable. Jackass has another more obscure meaning: moonshine. Jackass whiskey allegedly got its name because it had a bite like a mule and a kick like a horse. Prohibition became the law of the land on January 16, 1920. This ushered in the moonshining, or bootlegging, era that lasted 14 years until the Twenty-first Amendment repealed Prohibition on December 5, 1933.

During this time, rural ranches and farms became favorite places for moonshiners. Anne Marshall Homan writes in her 2001 book, *The Morning Side of Mount Diablo*: "During Prohibition years, many hardscrabble ranchers in the Black Hills [of Mount Diablo]—always strapped for ready cash—set up stills and secretly made

liquor besides their traditional wine." One such spot in Contra Costa County was in a remote canyon that local residents named "Jackass Canyon." Distilleries or stills were constructed in this canyon bottom because of the abundance of yearlong water from the west fork of Tassajara Creek. The creek was fed by an active spring that the moonshiners tapped by means of piping and a springbox. Armed sentries stood guard at strategic locations above the canyon to be on the lookout for Prohibition agents and robbers. The stills had the capability of making several hundred gallons of whiskey each day. It is interesting to note that one gallon of jackass whiskey would sell for approximately $5 in the 1920s.

JEREMIAH CREEK TRAIL
(T17)

JEREMIAH MORGAN STONE MEMORIAL MIKE WOODRING

This short creek was named for Jeremiah Morgan (see "Morgan Territory Road" place name).

JILL CREEK
(L15)

OLD SIGN AT JILL CREEK MIKE WOODRING

The creek is named for Jill Brumleve Kilcourse, granddaughter of Angel Kerley and daughter of Tom and Joan Brumleve (see "Angel Kerley Road" place name).

Jill Creek empties into Pine Canyon not far from the Diablo Ranch property.

JUNIPER TRAIL
(N14)

CALIFORNIA JUNIPER • *Juniperus californica*

CHARLES WEBBER

The California juniper *(Juniperus californica)* is a species of juniper found throughout the Park. This California native shrub or small tree is drought tolerant. The berry crops it produces annually are consumed by birds and mammals.

KNOBCONE POINT ROAD
(P17)

KNOBCONE POINT MIKE WOODRING

The knobcone pine *(Pinus attenuata)* is one of three California native pine trees indigenous to the Park. The other two are the coulter pine (see “Coulter Pine Trail” place name) and the gray pine *(Pinus sabiniana)*. The knobcone pine prefers dry, rocky environments, and is found exclusively on the road’s southwest exposure near the top. This pine has unique propagation capabilities; a fire is required to open the cones to distribute the seeds.

The "Point" refers to this area's highest rock promontory, elevation 1,810 feet.

On July 17, 2009, a beautiful redwood picnic table was placed by the Park in a secluded spot (about 1.5 miles from Curry Point) along Knobcone Point Road in memory of Kate McKillop (1936–2009). Kate was a longtime volunteer and benefactor for the Mount Diablo Interpretive Association and Save Mount Diablo. She died of natural causes on February 26, 2009. Kate's family and friends purchased the table through the California State Parks Foundation.

LAS TRAMPAS REGIONAL TRAIL
(115)

MIKE WOODRING

TRAIL SIGNPOST AT MACEDO RANCH

"Trampa" means "trap" or "snare" in Spanish. Hunters and fur trappers were the first non-Native-Americans to settle in Contra Costa County. Jedediah Smith, a well-known trapper, crossed Contra Costa County in May 1827.

LITTLE YOSEMITE TRAIL
(I14)

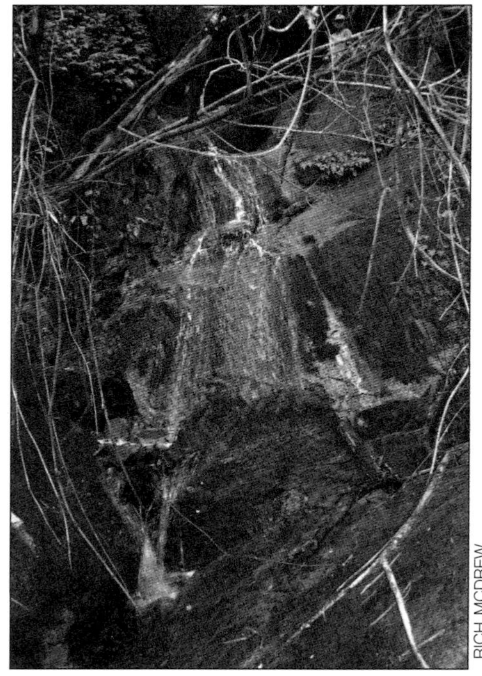

RICH MCDREW

FALLS ALONG TRAIL
(BURT BOGARDUS PICTURED AT TOP OF FALLS)

This trail was named because in the lower section within the Diablo Foothills Regional Park, there is a rocky creek edifice that looks like and performs like a miniature Yosemite Falls. Most of the year, no water flows in this drainage, but when it does flow after a hard rainstorm, it can be quite spectacular.

MACEDO RANCH
(115)

Frank A. Macedo (1886–1980) was a Portuguese immigrant from the Azores Islands. He arrived in New York City on a whaling vessel in 1903 and settled in Contra Costa County in 1906. In 1909, he purchased 825 acres around what is now the Mount Diablo State Park staging area in Danville. Frank grew hay, raised cattle and horses, and engaged in contract hay baling on farms in the area. In 1922, he leased 185 acres near downtown Walnut Creek and went into the dairy business, selling milk for 40 cents a gallon. He retired in 1945 to a home at 1835 Oakland Blvd., Walnut Creek. The Macedos sold their Danville property to the Park in 1959. Frank married Isabel Macedo in 1910. His wife and their only son, Frank Silviera Macedo (1912–1975), died the same year. The elder Frank died in Walnut Creek at the age of 94 and is buried in Holy Sepulchre Cemetery in Hayward.

MACEDO RANCH RICH MCDREW

MARSH TRAIL
(Q10)

CONTRA COSTA COUNTY HISTORICAL SOCIETY

JOHN MARSH'S "STONE HOUSE" IN 1866

Dr. John Marsh (1799–1856) owned a nearby ranch called "Los Meganos" (Spanish for "sand dunes"). He was the first American settler in Contra Costa County. John descended from an old New England family and was a graduate of Harvard College. In 1837, he obtained a grant from the Mexican government that contained 13,316 acres at the foot of Mount Diablo, now the geographic center of Contra Costa County. John married Abbie Tuch Marsh in 1851 and subsequently built the "Stone House" about four miles west of Brentwood. In 2002, the State of California acquired the 4,000-acre Cowell Ranch adjacent to the Stone House to create one of the newest parks in the State. John was brutally murdered and robbed on September 24, 1856, while driving his buggy on the road from one of his ranches in Martinez.

MARY BOWERMAN TRAIL
(O13)

DANN MCCRIGHT

MARY PHOTOGRAPHING THE MOUNT DIABLO FAIRY LANTERN *(Calochortus pulchellus)* C. 1990

Formerly the "Fire Interpretive Trail," it was renamed in honor of Dr. Mary Leolin Bowerman (1908–2005), who died on August 21, 2005. For nearly 75 years, Mary was considered the leading Mount Diablo botanist. She began studying the native plants of Mount Diablo for her doctorate dissertation at the University of California,

Berkeley, under the tutelage of the famed Dr. Willis Linn Jepson, Professor of Botany. This work was then turned into her first book published in 1944 entitled, *The Flowering Plants and Ferns of Mount Diablo, California*. Together with Barbara Ertter, she published an extended version in 2002. Mary co-founded Save Mount Diablo in 1971 with the charter of turning private property into parkland. Mary once said, "My dream is that the whole of Mount Diablo, including its foothills, will remain open space . . . so that the visual and natural integrity will be sustained." Mary was also one of the founding members of the Mount Diablo Interpretive Association in 1974.

MERIDIAN RIDGE ROAD
(N12)

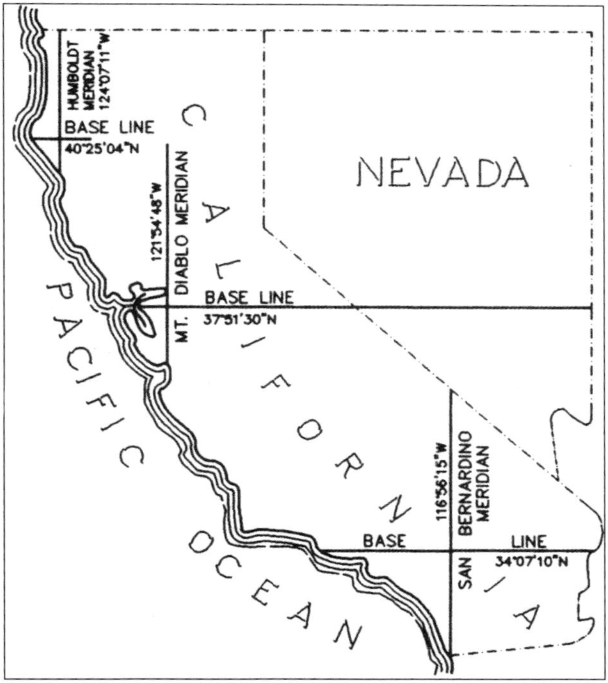

MOUNT DIABLO SURVEYORS HISTORICAL SOCIETY

CALIFORNIA/NEVADA SURVEY MAP

"Meridian" is a surveying term referring to the North-South axis lines drawn for land division. Some early maps name this road "Median Road."

MIMULUS SPRING
(O13)

MIKE WOODRING

MIMULUS SPRING—
NAMED FOR MONKEY FLOWER PLANT

GOLDEN MONKEYFLOWER
Mimulus guttatus
CALIFORNIA PLANT FAMILIES
BY GLENN KEATOR
UNIVERSITY OF CALIFORNIA PRESS, 2009
ILLUSTRATION BY
MARGARET (PEG) STEUNENBERG

The genus *Mimulus* is the Latin name for the monkeyflower plant. At least ten varieties of the monkeyflowers are found in Mount Diablo State Park. Some varieties are common around springs. "Mimulus Spring" was first identified on a map in Mary Bowerman's 1944 book, *The Flowering Plants and Ferns of Mount Diablo, California*, originally a doctoral dissertation. The second edition, updated with Barbara Ertter, was published in 2002 (see "Mary Bowerman Trail" place name).

MITCHELL CANYON ROAD
(L11)

MITCHELL CANYON TRAILHEAD RICH MCDREW

Isaac Mitchell (1829–1921) was a native of Kentucky. He came to Contra Costa County in 1849 with the gold rush and initially engaged in farming in the San Ramon Valley. He later purchased a large tract of land in the canyon where he lived until his death. He and his wife had six children. According to the authoritative *History of Contra Costa County*, published in 1926, "Mitchell Canyon, at the base of Mount Diablo, is named for him."

MIWOK ROAD
(R10)

BUNNER MCFARLAND, ARTIST | CONCORD HISTORICAL SOCIETY

BAY MIWOK OF CONTRA COSTA COUNTY

Miwok translates to "people" or "Indian people," and identifies any one of several different Native Californian groups. Native Californians lived in the area of Mount Diablo State Park for over 5,000 years before the arrival of the Europeans. The Bay Miwok tribelet, the Bolbon Indians (also known as Volvon/Wolwon), lived closest to Mount Diablo.

MORGAN CREEK ROAD
(U17)

MORGAN CREEK ROAD MIKE WOODRING

This Park fire road, which parallels Morgan Creek, is named for Jeremiah Morgan (see "Morgan Territory Road" place name).

MORGAN TERRITORY ROAD
(U17)

MORGAN TERRITORY ROAD RACHEL HAISLET

Both the "territory" and "road" were named for Jeremiah (Jerry) Morgan (1819–1906) and his descendants. Jeremiah was born in the Cherokee Nation, Alabama, near the Tennessee River. He came to California in 1849 and claimed 10,000 acres of land on "the morning side of Mount Diablo" in 1856. After the first official survey by the U.S. government in 1862, Jeremiah's land claims were reduced to 2,000 acres. Jeremiah had 16 children by his first wife, Sarah Ellis Morgan. She died in 1869. Morgan Territory Road was officially named by Contra Costa County in 1892. The road is 14.5 miles long and passes through four townships.

MOSES ROCK
(L13)

MOSES ROCK MIKE WOODRING

Water from a spring appears to seep out of the rock at this location. The name "Moses Rock" was coined because allegedly Moses (died around 1400 BC) produced water by striking a rock at Mount Horeb (Israel) with his staff. It is written in Exodus 17:6 that "I will stand there before you by the rock at Horeb. Strike the rock, and water will come out of it for the people to drink."

MOTHERS TRAIL
(L13)

NORTHERN END OF MOTHERS TRAIL — MIKE WOODRING

Named by Angel Kerley (see "Angel Kerley Road" place name) in honor of her mother, Angelina Toscani (1891–1975). Mrs. Toscani was born in California of Italian immigrants. She and her husband Anthony (1880–1967) had a son named Francis in addition to Angel. Anthony was born in Switzerland.

MOUNT DIABLO
(O13)

CONTRA COSTA COUNTY HISTORICAL SOCIETY

Five Martinez youths, in 1915, sit by the monument placed on the peak of Mount Diablo by State Surveyor Leander Ransom in 1851, when the peak was established as a base-meridian. They are, from left to right, Max Stinchfield, Hayden Davies, Morris Goldenzorff, William Edelman, and Hall Brillhart.

The origin of the name invokes speculation. The most popular version revolves around the Spanish word "Diablo" meaning "devil." This reference is believed to stem from an 1806 Spanish military expedition that went in search of runaway Native Californians from San Francisco's Mission Dolores. The Spanish soldiers caught sight of the runaways hiding in a willow thicket near what is now Buchanan Field in Concord and decided to wait until the next morning before capturing them. During the night, the group of Native Californians mysteriously escaped. In response, the Spanish dubbed the site "Monte del Diablo," meaning "Thicket of the Devil." Subsequently, English-speaking individuals believed "monte" translated to "mountain" and, thus, tagged the summit of the nearby mountain "Mount Diablo." Subsequent generations of visitors to the mountain thought the name to be appropriate because the trip to the summit was "a devil of a climb!"

MOUNTAIN HOUSE
(N15)

COURTESY OF THE CONTRA COSTA COUNTY HISTORICAL SOCIETY, C. 1954

SITE OF OLD MOUNTAIN HOUSE

The first and only hotel that was built on Mount Diablo was called "Mountain House." Built by Joseph Seavey Hall, it opened for business on May 4, 1874. Joseph Seavey Hall (1818–1899) was born on March 24 in Bartlett, New Hampshire, and was the third son (Joseph had nine brothers and one sister) of Reverend Elias, a Baptist preacher, and Hannah (nee Seavey) Hall. Actually, the Reverend Elias had 18 children by four wives. At the age of 26, Joseph married Sarah J. Crawford (1822–1869) in Vermont on March 19, 1845.

Joseph was one of the most active guides in the White Mountains of New Hampshire and a pioneer entrepreneur and engineer on Mount Washington. In 1852, Joseph Hall partnered with L.M. Rosebrook and built a hotel in the White Mountains in forty days near the summit of Mount Washington (elevation 6,288 feet). They called it "Summit House." The *Ballou's Pictorial* of August 9, 1856, reported that "the structure is of heavy stones, blasted with powder from the mighty pyramid on which it stands. It is 24 by 64 feet, secured to its foundation by cement and heavy iron bolts, while the roof is tightened by four strong cables." Mount Washington has the ominous distinction of clocking the highest surface wind speeds ever recorded on earth at 231 miles per hour on April 12, 1934. The cables were a necessity! Hall and Rosebrook sold the Summit House in 1855.

In his early 40s, Joseph marched through Pennsylvania with the 11th Regiment, Vermont Volunteers, as a First Lieutenant, and fought in the Battle of Gettysburg.

In 1866, after the Civil War, Joseph and Sarah purchased a silver mining venture near Virginia City, Nevada. Shockingly, Sarah died in Nevada at the early age of 47. After her passing, Joseph traveled to California and the Bay Area. He learned of the spectacular views and unique beauty of Mount Diablo and envisioned a hotel near its summit, much like his elevated hostelry experience at Mount Washington. But first, a road had to be built to the hotel—the hotel being planned on a flat spot about two miles below the Mount Diablo summit.

On October 30, 1873, Hall convened a meeting to organize the project of building two roads to reach the Mountain House, one from Pine Canyon in Ygnacio Valley, and one from Danville via Green Valley. The companies to create these roads at a cost of $22,000 were called the "Mount Diablo Summit Road Company," and the "Green Valley and Mount Diablo Summit Road Company." The directors of these "companies" were Joseph Hall, S.W. Johnson, W.W. Cameron, N. Jones, and John Slitz. W.W. Bagester surveyed the roads beginning on November 20, 1873. A right-of-way was purchased from James Walker, a well-known Walnut Creek rancher, who owned 1,400 acres on Mount Diablo. On December 31, 1873, Joseph purchased 23 acres from James Walker and S.W. Levy—the proposed site of the Mountain House. Construction of the hotel went rather quickly. On May 2, 1874, the two roads were officially opened and began carrying visitors twice daily in stagecoaches and carriages (see "Stage Road" place name photos) to the Mountain House.

In 1873, Joseph Hall married Julia F. Betts (1831–1887). Julia gave birth to Joseph's only child, Josa Sarah Hall, on July 5, 1874, at the Mountain House. On August 2, 1874, Joseph wrote the following to his siblings in New Hampshire (excerpted from a letter courtesy of William P. "Bill" Hall of Essex, Vermont—Joseph is Bill's great grand uncle): "Our house is located on the Mount Diablo Summit Road, the road I built; it is very pleasantly located surrounded by large oak trees and is very favorably located to accommodate visitors to the mountain. We have but 11 rooms, but near the house a large tent 40 feet wide with good floor and beds arranged to accommodate 20 people. We can accommodate 20 in the house but seldom have more than 20 to sleep overnight, but occasionally we have 40; over 2000 persons have passed over our road since it was opened the 1st of May; but for the last two weeks not so many as before owing to heavy fogs in San Francisco, but we expect a great travel in September and October, and to continue until the rainy season sets in. This is unlike Mount Washington. It is warmer here than in the valleys, and the land though very uneven will produce any kind of crops that are raised in the valleys and particularly adapted to fruit grapes figs peaches etc. etc. The view from Mount Diablo is the best and most extensive in the U.S if not the world overlooking as it does 25,000 square miles unobstructed and unlike Mount Washington, a good view can be had nearly every day of the year except through the rainy season. Our road is better than the Mount Washington summit road and easier kept in repair. We have had a good number of Eastern visitors and all are delighted with the visit."

Joseph installed a tent with a wooden floor at the top of the mountain so guests could stay at the summit overnight.

On a fall day in 1877, John Muir hiked Mount Diablo and overnighted at the summit "on a sheltered nook in the chaparral." Muir continued in a letter to friends dated December 5, 1877, about the next morning: "The sunrise was truly glorious. After lingering an hour or so, observing and feasting and making a few notes, I went down to that halfway hotel for breakfast." (excerpted from *The Life and Letters of John Muir*, 1924)

In 1878, Joseph ran into financial problems; consequently the Mountain House and the telescope were sold to Margaret Sloan, who with her son Horace, continued the operation for another 14 years. In 1884, Joseph and his family eventually settled in Frankfort, Michigan, where he was involved in logging the next ten years. Julia died there in 1887. Joseph returned to Vermont in 1894 and married Calista Fay, a schoolteacher in Hardwick, Vermont. Joseph died in Hardwick at the age of 81.

Unfortunately, a large wildfire scorched the summit of Mount Diablo in the summer of 1891. Consequently, visitation to the Mountain House dropped significantly, so Mrs. Sloan shuttered the hotel.

What happened to Josa Sarah Hall? She married Frank Stone in California. They had twin girls, Rachel and Ruth.

In 1901, the Mountain House burned completely, so nothing physical remains today. We know where it was located, and a wayside panel now marks its spot today, as one did beginning in 1954, one-quarter mile above the Junction Ranger Station on the Summit Trail.

MUIR PICNIC AREA
(N14)

LIBRARY OF CONGRESS

JOHN MUIR WITH PRESIDENT THEODORE ROOSEVELT
GLACIER POINT, YOSEMITE VALLEY, 1903

John Muir (1838–1914), American naturalist and explorer, was born in Dunbar, Scotland, and educated in Scotland and the University of Wisconsin. While traveling on foot, he visited many of the grander scenes in the mountains of California, including Mount Diablo in 1877. Founder of the Sierra Club, he was a pioneer advocate of forest conservation and establishment of national parks.

MURCHIO ROAD
(M9)

MURCHIO ROAD RACHEL HAISLET

Dominic Murchio (1849–1916) and his wife Julia Raggi Murchio (1859–1931) were born amid the vine-clad hills of sunny Italy. They were married in California in 1879 and settled in the Clayton area, becoming owners of one of the finest ranches in that area. The ranch extended up Mitchell Canyon to Deer Flat and included White Canyon. They grew hay, grain, and wine grapes and raised cattle on about 4,000 acres. Dominic and Julia were parents of 13 children. The Murchio family ranched in the Mitchell Canyon vicinity for almost 80 years.

OLD FINLEY ROAD
(T17)

OLD FINLEY ROAD MIKE WOODRING

Harrison Finley (1837–1918) was a native of Missouri and arrived in Contra Costa County in 1863. He initially leased land in Tassajara Valley. In 1875, he purchased 1,080 acres in Tassajara Valley where he farmed and raised livestock. He and his wife, Lavina Roy Finley (1849–1945), had eight children, all of whom were born in Contra Costa County. In 1888, the family relocated to Sonoma County.

OLOFSON RIDGE ROAD
(J11)

MIKE WOODRING

COAST HORNED LIZARD ON OLOFSON RIDGE ROAD • *Phrynosoma coronatum*

The Olofson family, John Peter Olofson (1834–1903) and his wife Clarissa Olofson (1840–1913) and their seven children, homesteaded 138 acres in the vicinity of Mitchell Canyon beginning in 1886. John emigrated from his native Stockholm, Sweden, at age 14. He arrived in San Francisco in 1848 and worked as a dockworker. He married his wife in 1857. She emigrated from Liverpool, England.

OLYMPIA TRAIL
(O11)

“Olympus,” the mountain throne of the Greek gods, and “Olympia,” the site of the Olympic Games, repeatedly have been used for American place names. Such is probably the case here. However, local legend persists that Mount Olympia was named for “Olympia Beer.” Before the area was annexed to Mount Diablo State Park, the Concord/Mount Diablo Trail Ride Association built many of the trails around Mount Olympia. The Association’s trail builders supposedly stashed Olympia beer along the trail to refresh themselves after a hard day’s work. Today, alcohol is not permitted in the Park. Leopold Schmidt founded Olympia Brewing Company in Tumwater, Washington, in 1896. Since 1983, it adopted the enduring slogan: “It’s the Water.” Unfortunately for beer drinkers, the last can of Olympia rolled off the line on May 27, 2003. Olympia Brewing Company is now history.

MOUNT OLYMPIA — MIKE WOODRING

OYSTER POINT TRAIL
(R19)

OYSTER POINT MIKE WOODRING

Oyster Point Trail leads to the vicinity of Oyster Point, elevation 2,106 feet. The trail and high point were named because the eroded rocks in the area reveal fossilized remains of oyster and crustaceous shells. Geologists theorize that millions of years ago all of Mount Diablo was many miles offshore. Through a process called "subduction," the ocean floor was uplifted to its present state. This is why the 191 million-year-old rocks are at the summit and the 100 million-year-old rocks are 3,000 feet lower on the mountain.

PERKINS CANYON
(Q12)

WATER STREAMING OVER THE HISTORIC DAM IN PERKINS CANYON

Solomon David Perkins (1822–1880) and his wife Susan (1830–1902), an influential farming family, owned land in the Morgan Territory area for ten years beginning in 1859. They had four children. He then moved his family to Tulare County. He and his entire family are buried at the cemetery in Visalia, California.

QUARRY ROAD
(Q11)

MINING FOR MERCURY ORE

MAE FIISHER PURCELL, *HISTORY OF CONTRA COSTA COUNTY*, DECEMBER 1940

Named for a mercury mine quarry that was at the end of this short gravel road. This surface mine quarry was operated by the Bradley Mining Company from October 1936 to January 1940. The CEO was Worthen Bradley.

QUICKSILVER TRAIL
(Q11)

QUICKSILVER TRAIL — MIKE WOODRING

Mercury mining, also known as quicksilver, dominated this area from as early as 1875 to 1940. Quicksilver deposits only occur in the Franciscan formation, i.e., serpentine and silica-carbonate rock, which is present in this vicinity. Mercury was extracted from tons of ore that was removed from underground and surface mines. It took a ton of ore to produce ten pounds of mercury.

RANSOM POINT
(O13)

RANSOM POINT FROM SUMMIT OBSERVATION DECK, 2004 RICH MCDREW

Leander Ransom (1800–1874), a U.S. Deputy Surveyor General, selected the summit of Mount Diablo as the base point to survey central California and western Nevada in the summer of 1851. He was born in Connecticut and while still a young man, went to Cleveland, Ohio. A few years later, he became President of the Public Works of Ohio and moved his family to Columbus. Leander was a man of imposing build, weighing 235 pounds and standing over six feet tall. He died at the

age of 74 as a result of an accident. As a fitting memorial to the pioneer work of Leander Ransom, the Society of Engineers dedicated "Ransom Point" near the Mount Diablo summit in October 1926. A few recent historical references, including previous editions of the *Trail Map of Mount Diablo State Park*, spell Leander's last name "Ransome." However, the more authoritative historical documents of his day spell his last name without the "e."

RAY MORGAN ROAD
(R12)

RAY MORGAN ROAD MIKE WOODRING

Raymond H. Morgan (1933–1986) lived in the Morgan Territory area. He served as the Fire Chief of the East Diablo Fire Protection District for 12 years and worked for this District for 26 years. Ray died in Clayton at the age of 53. His wife Helen, daughters Debra Finn and Renae Tharp, both of Antioch, parents Howard and Grace Morgan of Clayton, brother Ken Morgan of Napa, and two grandchildren, survived him.

RED ROAD
(K11)

RED ROAD MIKE WOODRING

Named because the surface soil in this area has a reddish color.

RHINE CANYON
(P14)

RHINE CANYON CLAYTON HISTORICAL SOCIETY

Charles Rhine (1838–1920), native to Poland, came to Contra Costa County in 1857 and opened a general merchandise store with partner Joel Clayton (see "Clayton Oaks Road" place name) near the present town of Clayton. He also owned and operated a 900-acre farm in the area. Most of the foodstuffs he raised he sold in his store. Charles also served as the postmaster in Clayton. In 1868, he married Celia Lobree Rhine, a native of Prussia. They had eight children. It is believed that the nearby "Rhyne [sic] Quicksilver Mine" was also named for him. It operated as far back as 1875 and helped to turn the tiny community of Clayton into a thriving town. Deposits of the red cinnabar became a valuable source of mercury for the country's munitions industry.

RIGGS CANYON ROAD
(T18)

RIGGS CANYON MIKE WOODRING

The canyon is named for Kentucky native Louisa Riggs Morgan (1829–1917) and her ancestors who owned property and raised livestock in the Canyon area in the mid-1800s. Louisa was Jeremiah Morgan's (see "Morgan Territory Road" place name) second wife. They were married in 1869. They had one son and were married for 37 years. She died in Modesto at age 88.

SATTLER TRAIL
(R10)

SATTLER TRAIL CROSSING DUNN CREEK MIKE WOODRING

This trail is named for William Henry Sattler (1909–1997) and his wife, Genevieve Sattler (1915–1999). For two decades, "Bill" and "Gen" were the quiet strength of Save Mount Diablo (SMD), the land trust they helped start in 1971. Bill was the Treasurer of SMD for almost two decades, and Gen was the Secretary. They both played a sentinel role in protecting the rugged open spaces of Mount Diablo from housing tracts. In l971, just 7,500 acres were protected as part of Mount Diablo State Park. Now, the Park's acreage exceeds 20,000 acres. Bill and Gen were married in 1950 and raised four children: Joyce, Carol, Edward, and Albert. Bill was a partner in Sattler's Appliance Stores (Concord) for 32 years. The business closed in 1990.

SENTINEL ROCK
(M17)

SENTINEL ROCK (SHARYN FERNANDEZ, PICTURED) DENNIS GALLOWAY

This promontory is a favorite destination for those who visit the Rock City area of the Park. This large boulder is made of massive sandstone. Even though the sandstone is hard enough to have resisted weathering until now, notice that people's feet and carving tools have left their mark. Years of playful climbing has worn smooth paths over this rock and others in the area. In the 1930s the Civilian Conservation Corps (see the "Civilian Conservation Corps Trail" place name) chiseled steps in the rock, and installed safety railings to aid people to reach the top of this rock. The steps and railings are there today.

SHARKEY ROAD
(Q10)

MAE FISHER PURCELL, *HISTORY OF CONTRA COSTA COUNTY* DECEMBER 1940

SENATOR SHARKEY

This fire road is named for California State Senator William R. Sharkey (1879–1948). Senator Sharkey authored and sponsored the 1921 California legislature bill that made Mount Diablo a State Park and Game Refuge in 1921. In addition to his role in politics, Senator Sharkey was well known as a newspaper publisher and conservationist.

SOTO SPRING
(J12)

SOTO SPRING RICH MCDREW

The spring is named for the de Soto family who owned and operated a 360-acre working cattle ranch east of North Gate Road for several generations. The de Soto ownership can be traced to the late 1800s to Alvarado John de Soto (1858–1916). Alvarado was a prominent political figure in Contra Costa County, serving as auditor for many years until 1907. His father, Silverio Ygnacio Carlos de Soto (1831-1906), was the grandson of Ignacio de Soto (1740-1807) of Sinaloa, Mexico. Ygnacio came to California in 1776 with the expedition of Captain

Juan Bautista de Anza and helped build the presidio and mission at San Francisco. It is important to note that Alvarado's brother, Presentación Marcus de Soto (1859–1932), a Concord postmaster for nearly 30 years, has been credited as the first person to work toward Mount Diablo becoming a State Park. Upon Alvarado's death, his children inherited the property and sold it to a realtor in the 1950s. Save Mount Diablo purchased the property in 1984 and subsequently deeded it to Mount Diablo State Park.

STAGE ROAD
(J14)

CONTRA COSTA COUNTY HISTORICAL SOCIETY

Seeley Bennett's stage in front of Hough's Hotel in Martinez, ready to leave for its daily trip to the top of Mount Diablo. Special stages, for the Mount Diablo run, were built by the Kimball Company of San Francisco.

On September 15, 1877, Seeley J. Bennett advertises his stage line through Ygnacio Valley, in the *Contra Costa Gazette*. This is not the first but is one of a continuing series of advertisements.

On November 4, 1873, the Mount Diablo Summit Road Company was incorporated to build a road from Ygnacio Valley in Walnut Creek, through Pine Canyon, and up to the summit. The "Stage Road" was opened on May 2, 1874, with two stage lines running twice daily from the Pacheco-Martinez area.

SYCAMORE CREEK ROAD
(O18)

CALIFORNIA SYCAMORE • *Platanus racemosa*

Named for the western or California sycamore tree *(Platanus racemosa),* which is found along this fire road and along banks of streams in the Park. It is a California native deciduous tree and can grow to lofty proportions, typically reaching a height of 75 feet as it struggles to find more sunlight. The sycamore tree is easily recognized by its whitish and blotched exfoliating bark.

TASSAJARA CREEK TRAIL
(S17)

TASSAJARA CREEK MIKE WOODRING

This name originates from the Spanish-American word "tasajero" ("tasajo" in Spanish means "jerked beef" or "piece of meat") designating a place where beef or venison is cut in strips and hung out in the sun to dry or cure.

THREE SPRINGS ROAD
(Q10)

THREE SPRINGS ROAD MIKE WOODRING

Named by Robert "Bob" Nunn, who owns five acres surrounded by parkland at the end of Three Springs Road (see "Wise Road" place name). Three active springs exist in the immediate vicinity of the Nunn property: Bay, Maple, and Walnut. Nunn legally draws his residential water from Maple Spring, which is atop Ridgeline Trail.

TICK WOOD TRAIL
(N10)

© 2006 JOYCE GROSS

WESTERN BLACK-LEGGED WOOD TICK
Ixodes pacificus

Named for the western black-legged tick *(Ixodes pacificus)* commonly found throughout the Park. At least two other species of ticks can also be found in the Park. Please be assured that there are not any more nor fewer ticks on this trail than other trails in the Park. There is another species called Rocky Mountain wood tick *(Dermacentor andersoni)*, but they are not normally found in California. This trail is not named after the very hard carving wood named "tick wood" or ebony wood, as this wood is only found in Africa and the Far East. So, it is believed that this trail was incorrectly named after the Rocky Mountain wood tick, and the words were inverted. However, the name "Tick Wood Trail" was created 20 years ago and is now part of the lore of the Park.

FOOTNOTE: The western black-legged tick is mostly active during the spring, summer, and fall seasons. Ticks are

difficult to avoid, especially on single-track trails, because hikers will inevitably brush up against foliage that the ticks are on. Ticks do not jump, but if one comes in contact with grass or shrubs, they will hitch a ride on one's clothing. The tick then proceeds to crawl to the nearest exposed skin where it begins the process of burrowing its head deep enough into one's tissue to reach blood. If you find a tick, use tweezers to grab the tick as close to your skin as possible, then pull the tick firmly, straight out, away from the skin (do not jerk, twist, or burn the tick). If you believe it has been attached to your skin for at least 24 hours, ask your doctor about taking antibiotics as an insurance against infection.

The best defense against tick bites is to wear light-colored long-sleeved shirts and long pants tucked into socks. The light-colored clothing allows one to see that these critters have hitched a ride, and just flick them off your clothing with your finger.

TOYON PICNIC AREA
(N15)

TOYON, CHRISTMAS BERRY • *Heteromeles arbutifolia*

Named for the toyon *(Heteromeles arbutifolia)*, commonly named Christmas berry and California holly, which is a common perennial shrub native to California. The bright red berry-like fruit are consumed by birds as well as mammals. The seeds are dispersed by such wildlife. Toyon berries were gathered by Native American tribes many centuries ago. The berries were roasted over open coals or boiled in a cooking basket to take away the bitter taste of the fresh fruit. The name "Toyon" is believed to be of Native American origin.

TRAIL THROUGH TIME (N17)

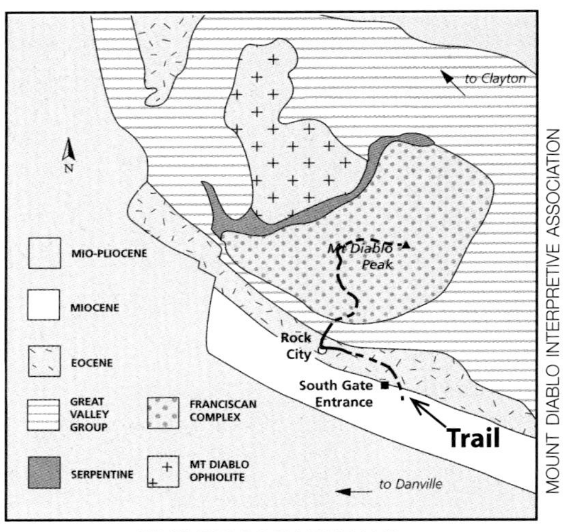

TRAIL THROUGH TIME MAP

The Trail Through Time is a 6.25-mile hiking route on the south side of Mount Diablo from the Park boundary on Sycamore Creek Road on the south to the Mary Bowerman Trail near the summit of the mountain. The name of the route reflects its journey past geologic rocks from the youngest at the south end to the oldest rocks at the summit with an age of 190 million years. Twenty interpretive panels have been placed at key locations along the route to illustrate, using text and graphics, interesting geologic features and other items of historical and botanical value.

For the most part, the Trail Through Time uses existing fire roads and single-track trails along its route. Only one section of new trail had to be constructed for the route, that connecting Lower Rock City on the west to Devils Slide Trail on the east. A free self-guiding color brochure is available at certain panels. The brochure has a map of the route, a brief summary of each panel, and other pertinent information. The complete route has a vertical elevation gain of 2,940 feet. It can also be traversed in reverse down the mountain walking over older to younger rocks. It is important to mention that the panels are independent of each other, and therefore shorter segments of the route can also provide an informative geologic experience.

TURTLE ROCK RANCH
M15

TURTLE ROCK MIKE WOODRING

This 65.5-acre picnic resort is named after a large rock formation resembling a turtle. This reptilian resemblance is composed of radiolarian chert that sits among massive Franciscan boulders behind the gate to Diablo Ranch.

Originally known as Rancho Miguel, present-day Turtle Rock Ranch was part of the 17,782-acre Mexican land grant accorded to Doña Juana Sanchez de Pacheco on July 31, 1834. The Rancho Arroyo de las Nueces y Bolbones (Creek of the Walnuts and Indians) grant also included

Pine Canyon, Little Pine Canyon, and the North Gate Road area and Diablo Ranch.

The house and property, now known as Turtle Rock Ranch, was the original headquarters of Diablo Ranch (see "Angel Kerley Road" place name). In 1948, the Turtle Rock Ranch area was sold to a developer who created an exclusive recreation resort for large group functions. Over the next 30-plus years, ownership changed several times.

In 1981, Mitch and Ann Ward, local schoolteachers, bought the land. They operated a seasonal family business for 19 years, serving approximately 30,000 meals each summer. Located on the western slope of Mount Diablo, the ranch invited over 500,000 visitors to enjoy the views of central Contra Costa County, Walnut Creek, and Suisun Bay.

In September 1997, the Wards approached the State about the property in order to protect it from development. After two years of negotiation between the Department of Parks and Recreation, Save Mount Diablo, California State Senator Richard Rainey, and Assembly Member Lynne Leach, Turtle Rock Ranch was purchased from the Wards for $1.745 million and added to Mount Diablo State Park.

This area is not yet open to the public except for special events.

TWIN PEAKS
(M10)

TWIN PEAKS MIKE WOODRING

Above Mitchell Rock on the Mitchell Rock Trail are two distinct rock promontories that reach an altitude of 1,733 feet—a 1,133-foot increase in elevation from the Mitchell Canyon parking lot. This type of rock is called "diabase,"a dark gray igneous rock (rock solidified from a melt) similar to basalt. From Mitchell Rock and Twin Peaks looking northwest, one can see below at the edge of Clayton a 435-acre diabase quarry owned by CEMEX, a large Mexican company. This surface mine has been chipping away at Mount Zion for over 50 years. The mine produces crushed rock for building and roadbed foundations and materials for ready-mix concrete.

UNCLE SAM CANYON
(L1O)

It is believed that this canyon was named by miners in the early 1900s. The name was very popular with prospectors at the time, as the name appears on other natural locations throughout California and other states.

LIBRARY OF CONGRESS
UNCLE SAM CARTOON

Uncle Sam is the cartoon embodiment of the government of the United States, a character who appeared in newspapers and magazines beginning in the first part of the 19th century. The commonly accepted version of his origin, or at least the best explanation anyone has been able to supply, is that he was modeled after Samuel Wilson (1766-1854), a meat purveyor to the United States Army during the War of 1812. Known as "Uncle Sam," Wilson put his initials on his goods. The initials U.S. were also taken to stand for United States. Over the years, Uncle Sam evolved into a tall white-haired man with beard, sporting patriotic colors and a top hat. The most common modern image can be traced to his depiction by artist James Montgomery Flagg (1877–1960) in 1916, for a military recruitment poster calling, "I Want YOU for the U.S. Army."

WALKER CANYON
(I11)

WALKER HOME C.1879 WALNUT CREEK HISTORICAL SOCIETY

James Toomey Walker (1825–1902) and his family were early settlers in the Walnut Creek area. James married Mary Caroline Vaughan Walker (1840–1922) in 1861. They had a son and two daughters. In 1868, he built a home on his 1,400-acre ranch (acquired in 1851). The home remains today on North Gate Road in Walnut Creek at the foot of Mount Diablo State Park.

James' famous uncle, Joseph Reddeford Walker (1798–1876), moved into the new house with his nephew

and lived there until his death at the age of 77. Joseph Reddeford Walker was a trapper, trailblazer, guide, and stock buyer of the 1830s and 1840s. Walker Pass in the Sierra Nevada is named for him. He is buried in Alhambra Cemetery in Martinez, where his headstone recounts the highlights of his career. James' son, John "Johnnie" Walker (1862–1942), remained on the ranch after his father's death. He continued in the cattle business for almost three decades. At one time, his herd numbered over 1,500 cattle. John married Margaret McDonald Walker in 1886. They had seven children, all born on the ranch established by James.

WALNUT TRAIL
(T18)

WALNUT TREE • *Juglans californica* © 2003 BON TERRA CONSULTING

Named for the California black walnut tree or Hinds black walnut tree *(Juglans californica* or *hindsii)* at the junction of this trail and Old Finley Road. It is a large single-trunked deciduous tree up to 60 feet tall. It grows in stream beds and riparian woodlands. An active year-round spring is near these trees. The California black walnut tree is included in the California Native Plant Society's inventory of rare and endangered plants. This is one of the few remaining stands in the Park.

WASSERMANN TRAIL
(O10)

PHOTO COURTESY OF DR. FRANZ WASSERMANN

FRANZ AND SARAH READY FOR A RIDE IN 1963

This trail is named for Dr. Franz W. Wassermann and his wife Sarah Wassermann. Both Franz and Sarah were 83 years old in 2004 and live in Walnut Creek. He was born in Munich, Germany, and she in Cleveland, Ohio. They joined the Concord/Mount Diablo Trail Ride Association in 1960 and have been very active with the Association's operations and events since then. For many years, Franz was a psychiatrist with Contra Costa County and also in private practice. They have two children: Paul, a pediatrician in Chico, and Margie Bone, a psychiatrist in Seattle. The Trail Ride Association named the trail for Franz and Sarah before the land was annexed to Mount Diablo State Park.

WILDCAT TRAIL
(M16)

BOBCAT • *Lynx rufus*

GERALD AND BUFF CORSI © 1999
CALIFORNIA ACADEMY OF SCIENCES

Two indigenous wildcats live in the Park: the bobcat *(Lynx rufus)* and the mountain lion *(Felis concolor)*. Unlike the mountain lion, the bobcat is commonly observed. It has a gray to brown coat, whiskered face, and black-tufted ears, and is about twice the size of a domestic cat. The bobcat derives its name from a black-tipped stubby tail. Largely solitary, it will hunt anything from insects to small deer, but prefers rabbits and rodents. Each night the bobcat will move from 2 to 7 miles along its habitual route. An estimated 50 bobcats inhabit Mount Diablo State Park. The trail and nearby camp are named for the bobcat.

WISE ROAD
(Q10)

WISE ROAD MIKE WOODRING

Dr. Warren R. Wise (1909–1989) and his family owned a house and 83 acres along this road from 1934 to the early 1990s. Warren was a medical doctor who worked for Johns Manville International in Pittsburg, California. Robert Nunn purchased this property, also known as "Three Springs," from the Wise heirs. Robert kept the house on 5 acres and sold the remaining 78 acres to Save Mount Diablo in 1992. This property was then deeded to the State of California to be included in Mount Diablo State Park.

WRIGHT CANYON
(R14)

COURTESY OF DOROTHY WRIGHT

MARTIN AND DOROTHY WRIGHT

Dorothy Tudder Wright named the canyon in memory of her late husband, Martin Barr Wright (1920–1999) and his ancestors and descendants. Dorothy and Martin were high school sweethearts in Oakland, and were married in 1942. In 1946, they purchased 110 acres along Morgan Territory Road for $20,000 from the Olofson family estate. Martin's parents were George Ross Wright (1892–1958) and Edith Olofson Wright (1893–1992). Edith was a granddaughter of John Peter and Clarissa Olofson (see "Olofson Ridge Road" place name). Dorothy and Martin owned and operated Curry Creek Park from 1946 to 1981 and raised five children.

ZIPPE TRAIL
(P11)

TRAIL SIGNPOST WORK CREW ALONG ZIPPE TRAIL, 1995 RICH MCDREW
L–R: PAUL BENNETT, UNKNOWN, HARVEY BROSLER, RICH MCDREW, BURT BOGARDUS

Emmett Wilbur Zippe (1906–1987) owned and resided on 535 acres on the north slope of Mount Diablo. His property was deeded to the Park in 1978. Emmett was an employee of Pacific Bell. He died in Contra Costa County at the age of 80.

MOUNTAIN LORE INDEX